Anchoring in the Storm

A Journey to Easter

Josh Ross

ISBN: 9798701167375

All Scripture quotations, unless otherwise indicated, are taken from the Holy Bible, New International Version. Copyright ©1973, 1978, 1984, 2011 by Biblica, Inc. Used by permission of Zondervan. All rights reserved worldwide. www.zondervan.com The "NIV" and "New International Version" are trademarks registered in the United States Patent and Trademark Office by Biblica, Inc.

Some names and dates in this book have been changed to protect the privacy of individuals.

Chapter 3, *Resting in the Storm*, and Chapter 4, *Walking Over the Storm* derive from content in Chapter 8 of *Scarred Hope*, written by Beverly and Josh Ross. You can purchase *Scarred Hope* from Amazon.com, or you can contact Wise County Christian Counseling: www.wiseccc.org.

Front and back cover design by Justin Ardrey.

Editor: Jenna King

Anchor strong!

To my dad, Rick Ross,
You have been an anchor for our family.
You broke cycles.
You have allowed God to restore broken parts of you.
You have navigated many storms in your life.
You have modeled loyalty through them all.
Thank you

Contents

ANCHORING IN THE STORM

INTRODUCTION

"You just got 2020'd!"

It's a phrase we will use for years to come when someone stubs their toe, has a flat tire, or the hot water heater goes out at home. 2020 has marked us. It may take time for us to remember formidable events that happened in 2004 or 2013, but we will always remember what 2020 brought to the world. Stories will be told about where we quarantined, what masks we wore, social unrest that transpired, a toxic presidential election, and how sports were played in front of empty stadiums.

The year 2020 has expanded our vocabulary. Words like coronavirus, pandemic, zoom, and pivot are used by us all. Phrases such as "safer-at-home," "virtual school," "hybrid church," "physical distancing," "mask-up," and "unmute yourself" have become familiar to us in everyday life.

2020 can be described as a crisis, or maybe better stated, a storm. The seasons of the year came in waves. Surges weren't constant, but they were steady. Some tried to deny the existence of the storm, but the impact has been felt by us all. We have lost people, dreams, plans, and things. We have gained perspective and the joy of embracing each day as a gift. 2020 has had its way with us.

Throughout life, we don't ask for storms. We don't invite them into our plans. They come whether we send invitations for them or not.

1

The question isn't, "How do we avoid storms?" But rather, "How do we prepare to be anchored well *now*, so that we are ready when they come?"

***

In September, my family planned a big celebration for my 40th birthday. We took the boys out of school, jumped in a rental car, and went south to the beach. A few sunny days in Florida would be a great way to unwind after a long year and to break in a new decade of life.

As we drew near to the coast, we began to notice on weather apps and social media platforms that a tropical storm was making its way to the Louisiana coast. The last time we went to Florida our trip was cut short by a tropical storm and we were determined to not let such a storm stop our trip again. We planned to hunker down, anticipating we would get a little wind and rain and hopeful that it wouldn't impact our trip that much.

Over the next 48 hours, we watched as the storm slowly swerved closer and closer toward Florida. It was no longer going to hit Louisiana, and it was no longer a tropical storm. Hurricane Sally had developed into a category two hurricane that was now heading straight to where we were staying. As we discerned whether to leave or not, we were informed by others in our condo that they had closed the bridge that connects the strip to the mainland. A decision had been made for us. There was no way to leave. We hunkered down.

For those of you familiar with the enneagram, I am a seven and Kayci is a six. This means that I am an enthusiast. I'm always up for an adventure. The more risks, the better. I knew this condo had endured multiple hurricanes over the years, and never had a window been broken. I figured our chances of survival were high, and for the rest of our lives we could tell the story of how we stared a category two hurricane in the face and didn't back down.

On the other hand, Kayci, as a six, is loyal to her people and is a worst-case-scenario thinker. She went into survival mode: How do we protect the kids, where do we hide, and where do I leave a goodbye letter for others to find because we may not make it?

Well, as you can safely assume, we survived. I fully acknowledge that while we can laugh about our experience, Hurricane Sally took a few lives and caused millions of dollars in damage. Storms don't care about the damage they leave behind. Compassion, sensitivity, and empathy aren't character traits they possess.

If you don't live near a coastline, you'll probably never face the devastating impact of a hurricane. Yet, most of us will endure countless thunderstorms throughout our lives.

Storms come in many different shapes and sizes. As we persevered through COVID, it felt like a storm that just wouldn't let up. Other storms have come in the form of cancer diagnoses, car wrecks, waves of depression, losing loved ones, divorce, job loss, pay cuts, and chronic pain. We have all faced those seasons of life when it feels like you're in a car stuck under a downpour, the windows won't roll up, and you can't see out the front windshield.

***

Now, you can read this book any time throughout the year and hopefully gain insight, inspiration, and values worth embracing as you navigate the storms of life. However, I wrote this as a gift to the Sycamore View Church and to others as a unique way to think about the season leading up to Easter. A few months ago, I realized that the spring of 2021 will most likely be the only spring that we will be fully immersed in COVID. In 2020, the virus hit in full force mid-March, and hopefully in 2022 we will be able to live life on the other side of the pandemic. Yet, in 2021, we anticipate this being a season of longing for change, yet wading through the flood waters as we get closer to solid ground.

No matter what season of life we are in, no matter what storms we find ourselves in the middle of, we are in need of anchoring. Hebrews 6:19 says, "We have this hope as an anchor for the soul, firm and secure."

A solid anchor won't protect us from the entirety of the storm, but it will provide stability, protection, security, and connection while in it. Without a solid anchor, we drift, get carried away, and lose our center. I want to encourage you to take seriously what it means to declare Jesus as an anchor for your soul right now in your life; not when you find yourselves in the middle of the storm. Prepare for waves of life before they come. Don't wait until you are in the storm to try to make preparations.

The story of Easter is a story of anchoring. No, I'm not talking about the Easter bunny, a new dress, and lots of chocolate. I'm talking about the story that has revolutionized the entire world. It's the story of unfathomable love, tremendous sacrifice, and life-changing courage. It's the story of Jesus; His adventurous life, death, burial, and resurrection. This is the story in which we are asked to be anchored. It's not a story of worship style, traditionalism, or what branch of Christianity you subscribe to, but a story of life in Jesus. In life, it's not just that you are anchored, but that you are anchored in the right story, or better said, anchored in the right person: Jesus.

I want to help us think about the season leading up to Easter as a journey. This isn't just arriving to a destination or to a belief system.

It's the journey of what it means to be human. It's the struggle we are always in while we live life on this earth. It's the struggle of darkness, light, sin, life, repentance, bondage, and freedom. I want to help us think of life as a variety of storms we must navigate, while never allowing the storms to define who we are. We must only allow Jesus to be the voice speaking identity and truth over us.

The journey to Easter is a journey of struggle. Every single year. It's the same struggle. It's the struggle of death to life.

***

Since early in the story of Christianity, many have called the season leading up to Easter "Lent." As Christianity became more and more non-Jewish, the church began taking very seriously what the conversion process meant for people. Easter Sunday became a day where many would be baptized following a 40-day journey of prayer, fasting, studying, and discerning. Conversion has always functioned best when it's both about what you are saying no to and what you're saying yes to. Surrendering a life to Jesus is meant to be a serious decision in which one is committing to a new way of life.

It takes surrendering your entire self to Jesus in order to live with Jesus as your primary anchor and primary lens with which to view the world. It will take hard work for the rest of your life to keep Jesus as your anchor and primary lens.

Growing up I thought Lent was only for Catholics, and those who I knew that honored Lent didn't seem to take it very seriously. I had a friend who would give up a particular kind of candy bar that they didn't even like and a friend who gave up pizza, but they hated pizza. In my mind, I thought of it more as a cultish practice than a spiritual one.

I began practicing the spiritual discipline of fasting when I was 19. At 21, I became more aware of practices that had shaped the church in the early years of Christianity. It reframed the season leading up to Easter as a passionate plea for meaningful, intentional discipleship. So, at the age of 21 I decided to give Lent a try. And I wasn't alone.

Kayci decided to walk through the season with me, as well as one of my best friends, Brandon Gilkey. Kayci and I were engaged to be married in May, so in March of that year, we began our journey to Easter. We knew we wanted Jesus to be the foundation of our marriage, so we wanted to use Lent as a season to set our hearts right. We devoted ourselves to intense seasons of prayer and repentance. We committed to reading through all four gospels and at least one Psalm per day. Our genuine plea was for God to use this season of prayer and fasting to grow our love for Jesus.

We decided to give something up for Lent, and because of how seriously we took our soon-to-be marriage covenant, we decided to go big. However, we probably should have thought this through a little better. I decided to give up meat and sodas for seven weeks. If you know anything about me, I love meat. I don't judge vegans and vegetarians, but I do like to point out that the sheet that came down in Peter's vision in Acts 10 didn't have salad, kale, or asparagus hanging over the edge of it.

I gave up meat. Kayci decided to give up desserts. Do you see how this was going to be a problem?

Our first dinner together once we entered into the season of Lent didn't go very well. I ordered soup and salad. Kayci ordered fajitas. I wasn't upset that she ordered meat, but I was a little taken back that she ordered a form of meat that you can hear sizzling from a mile away. Toward the end of our meal, the server asked if we would like any dessert. Kayci said, "No, sir. We are fine. Thank you." Yet, after watching her devour fajitas for thirty minutes, I quickly responded, "Yes we would. In fact, can you bring that dessert tray that has all of the options?" I proceeded to take my time staring at each piece of dessert before selecting my brownie with ice cream. We left the meal, shared a laugh together, and then we agreed that we would do better about honoring each other over the next few weeks.

That Easter was one of the most memorable Easters of both of our lives. We had courageously been anticipating a deep connection with God through our journey toward Easter. Easter was festive, celebratory, and full of hope. Yet, the journey up to Easter is what transformed our hearts. God used that season to sift out insecurities, unhealthy emotions, poor habits, and sin, and God brought us to life in deeper ways. We knew from that time on, Lent was going to be a part of our lives.

***

You may choose to do nothing this Lent season. Maybe I can convince you to use this book to help you reflect. If you do choose to fast from something, my advice would be to not overly commit and to not be overly ambitious. Fast from something that matters. Know that fasting is not meant by God to be a meaningless weight loss plan; it's meant to draw us closer to God. Have a plan of what your focus will turn toward when you begin to hunger for what it is you are choosing to abstain from.

I want to use a few stories of storms found through the Bible to guide us to Easter. I don't intend to spiritualize all of these stories to make them into spiritual storms in our lives today, though that will happen. I do intend to help us see the character, nature, and mission of God in each one, and how the mission of God keeps advancing no matter what.

The same God who saw people through storms in the past can do it again.

Often, the hardest step to take on a journey is the first one. Take a step with me. Let's journey together.

DUST AND ASHES

CHAPTER 1

It was my seventh grade Christmas party at school, and my girlfriend and I decided to exchange gifts during class. It was a pretty big deal. It's one thing to exchange gifts when you're outside of school, but the pressure is on when you choose to open each other's gift at the class Christmas party. She opened mine first, and while I don't remember what I got her, I think it's safe to say it was nothing short of breath-taking, or something like that. It could have been a golden necklace, a diamond ring, or quite possibly a Sweet Valley High book collection or a Boyz II Men poster. I seriously can't remember.

Then it was my turn to open her gift. I had dropped a hint earlier in the week that I was hoping to get an Atlanta Braves hat for Christmas. I was raised an Astros and Rangers fan, but the Braves had everyone's attention those days. I opened the gift, and sure enough, it was a ball cap. However, it wasn't an Atlanta Braves hat. It was close. It was a Cleveland Indians hat. She got her indigenous groups mixed up. She mistakenly and unintentionally got me an Indians hat thinking it was a Braves hat. Some would say this wasn't a big deal and that it's the thought that counts, but if she can't get her sport teams straight, what's next? I was left with no choice but to end the relationship. Or something like that.

Have you ever expected one thing in life, yet you got something else? There are those moments when expectations aren't met, or they are revealed as something we never saw coming.

For those of us who are followers of Jesus, we have surrendered to a story full of these moments. Think about it. Our story includes a virgin birth, a king from a little town called Bethlehem, a king who advocated for the poor and marginalized, and a Messiah who didn't come to usher in a national conquest, but rather implement an ethic of love and belonging that would take the world by storm. No one was expecting this kind of king or kingdom.

For most inductions into kingdoms or clubs throughout the history of the world, you must have money, wealth, influence, a lineage, a resume, recommendations from powerful people, or the willingness to perform at a level worthy of membership. Not so in the Kingdom of God. Entrance into this Kingdom means taking seriously confession, repentance, and complete surrender to this new way of life.

***

I want to talk about repentance, because it's often emphasized in conversion, but maybe not so much as a daily exercise to help us mature in our faith.

For nearly two decades of my life, as I have intentionally journeyed toward Easter, I have wrestled with the tension between winter and spring. For most of us, February ends with tension. Winter and spring collide, and there seems to be a few weeks when they arm wrestle to see who's going to win. I went to school at a college in Texas, and there were days when it would be 27 degrees in the morning and 72 in the afternoon. They just couldn't decide who was going to win.

Our walks of faith have these seasons where the cold, dark elements, and the light that is eager to bring new life are in tension with each other. All storms are because of tension. It's high pressure colliding with low pressure, eastern wind colliding with western wind, and warm temperatures colliding with the cold.

***

The season called Lent—this journey leading up to Easter—begins with a day called Ash Wednesday. You've probably heard of it before. Maybe all you knew about it is that it was the day you had a friend or co-worker who would show up with ashes on their forehead and you attempted to tell them they had something on their face. If you've ever done that before, please raise your hand right now.

I didn't know much about Ash Wednesday growing up, and what I did know was sort of confusing. It didn't make sense to me. But I also didn't grow up thinking much about the Christian calendar: Advent, Ash Wednesday, Lent, Easter, etc. They weren't really on my radar.

Here's what I believe now: you can be a mature Christian and never honor Lent or take the season leading up to Easter seriously. Heaven is going to be full of people who never put ashes on their foreheads and never fasted for a day in their lives. However, you can't be a mature Christian and not have serious, intentional, focused seasons of reflection in your life. Spiritual development will not happen without it.

M. Scott Peck writes, "Examination of the world without is never as personally painful as examination of the world within...yet when one is dedicated to the truth this pain seems relatively unimportant."[1]

I think he's right. We often avoid deep seasons of examination because we're afraid of what we'll find, or what God will expose. We want to rush to Easter, where we are greeted by victory, triumph,

---

[1] Marjorie Thompson, *Soul Feast* (Louisville, KY: Westminster John Knox Press, 1995), 83.

and eternal hope. Reflecting on death and repentance isn't going to gain a crowd, but it's the reality of the journey we are on. The victory of the empty tomb needs the solemn reminder of death and repentance that a day like Ash Wednesday brings.

Good, solid anchors need repentance which, throughout the Bible, often came in the form of ashes.

***

Ashes show up quite a bit in the Bible:

Genesis 3:19, "...for dust you are and to dust you will return."

Job 42:6, "Therefore I despise myself and repent in dust and ashes."

Daniel 9:3, "So I turned to the Lord God and pleaded with him in prayer and petition, in fasting, and in sackcloth and ashes."

Throughout the Bible, the phrase "sackcloth and ashes" is repeated as a reminder of mortality, repenting of sin, and interceding for other people.

When people were covered with ashes, it marked a point. Specifically, it marked a turning point. It was women and men of faith choosing to express themselves by saying things like, "I can't continue in this way any longer."

Repentance isn't only what you do when you choose to join the path with God. It's not simply a once-in-a-lifetime act in our conversion story. This may have been the way you heard about repentance when you grew up. Maybe you grew up thinking repentance was for conversion-moments and the big sins. Yet, repentance is something meant to be practiced every single day of our lives. It's what keeps us on track with God.

When God's children come before the throne of God in a posture of repentance, the voice from heaven doesn't speak, "It's about time," or, "I couldn't be more disappointed with you." Instead, heaven applauds. There is so much God can do with a repentant heart.

The journey to Easter begins with the reminder, "From dust you came, and to dust you will return."[2] It means that death is all around us. We can't escape death. As believers in Jesus, we believe death has been defeated and it will not get the final word, yet we also know death will one day have its way with us.

We rush to victory and hope, because no one wants to sit in ashes too long. Ashes aren't a dwelling place. It's not a permanent residence. Trust me, I know this all too well. As a seven on the enneagram, I avoid pain at all costs. The danger for sevens who are pastors is that when we are unhealthy, we tend to preach a lot more hope and resurrection than we do sacrifice and the cross. However, development and maturity happen when we sit in a season of reflection, not when we rush through it.

Dust and ashes aren't about misery. Instead, they give us a better vision of God.

Teresa of Avila says, "Stop thinking about your misery, insofar as possible, and turn your thoughts to the mercy of God, to how God loves us and suffered for us."[3]

---

[2] Genesis 3:19.

[3] *The Collected Works of St. Teresa of Avila*, Vol. II, trans. Kieran Kavanaugh and Otilio Rodriquez (Washington D.C.: Institute of Carmelite Studies, 1980), 190.

***

So, what about this whole "ashes on the forehead" thing?

You may never choose to participate in an Ash Wednesday service, but I hope you'll take seriously the need for the practice of repentance in your life. In the future, when you do see someone with ashes on their head, let me attempt to equip you how to talk with them about faith, instead of avoiding them because it looks weird.

Ashes on the head means that something is terribly wrong in the world.

Ashes on the head are also in the shape of the cross.

Ashes serve to remind us that we are sinners, deserving of death. The fact that they're in the shape of a cross reminds us that we have a Savior who willingly died to give us life.

In February of 2020, we hosted an Ash Wednesday service at Sycamore View and we called it a Night of Repentance. As I ended my message, I invited people to a few different places throughout the room. There were tables where people could write prayer requests or sins they needed to repent of in their lives. There was a table with candles that could be lit to symbolize the light that shines in our darkness. We had a table with communion, because any night of repentance can be a memorable moment to hold the bread and cup as we reflect on all that God has accomplished through Jesus.

And, for the first time in our church's existence, we offered a station in the back corner where people could go if they desired to have ashes placed on their heads. I was the person holding the ashes. I had the phrase ready to speak over anyone who chose to come, "From death you came, and to dust you will return. Repent, and believe the good news."

I'll be honest, I wasn't expecting many people to come to this station. Yet, immediately, up walked a friend. As I placed ashes on his head, I looked up, and to my surprise, there was a long line of people. Some stepped forward with tears flowing. Others closed their eyes, opened their hands, and received the moment as a divine connection with a God who was eager to dispense mercy. Some said how much they needed the moment, yet they knew if their Church of Christ relatives knew they received ashes at an Ash Wednesday service that there was no way they would be invited to Christmas.

It was a holy night. The grace of God was abundant.

A friend of mine, Cana Moore, a student at Harding School of Theology moved forward to receive ashes. She asked if I wanted her to place some on me. I declined, because in the moment, I had a job to do. I was in the moment to give, not receive.

However, at the very end of the night, it came over me, "Who are you to deny someone's request to mark you as one who is in need of God's mercy? Why would you refuse the blessing?"

So, I went over to Cana, and I asked her to place the ashes upon my forehead. She did, and I had a much-needed moment with God.

It was an anchoring moment for me. Often we anchor best not when we only focus on the anchor's strength, but when we take seriously how desperate we are to have it in our lives.

Repentance is a gift. Don't run from it. Practice it. Watch Jesus delight in the opportunity it gives God to grow you in ways you could never imagine.

THE SOUND NO STORM CAN SILENCE

CHAPTER 2

A few years ago, I was flying back to Memphis late one Saturday. I had connected at the DFW airport and the flight to Memphis is typically a little over an hour long. As we made our way over Arkansas, I moved to the window seat. I typically prefer an aisle seat, but I had an entire row to myself, and I could see lightning in the distance. I wanted to get a better look at it. It was one of the most gorgeous lightning storms I had ever seen. With each strike it lit up the sky. It was mesmerizing. I was returning from speaking at an event in which I had witnessed God transform lives. My heart was already full of gratitude, and my senses were alert to the majesty of God.

Something happened with this storm that I had never witnessed before because of where I was positioned. I wasn't looking up at a storm. I wasn't looking far in the distance at a storm. I was above it. It was below me. The clouds were in between me and the lightning bolts, so with each strike, it lit up the clouds beneath us. I couldn't see lightning bolts; I could only see clouds that lit up each time there was a strike. Now, I know lightning can be extremely dangerous, so my theology isn't that God is behind every lightning strike, yet there was something about this moment that was breathtaking, even sacred.

Then it hit me, if we were approaching Memphis, and there was a thunderstorm beneath us, somehow we had to get through a storm in order to land on the ground. I wasn't freaking out, but I did know that there was absolutely nothing I could do in the moment. I knew the pilot wasn't going to fly us through the eye of the storm, but I also knew that we were going to have to travel through part of the storm to land safely on the ground. I had to trust that the pilot had the training, wisdom, and expertise to navigate our plane through the obstacle in front of us.

I don't believe every storm we face in life is because God set it in motion. I do believe that every storm we face in life is a moment for God to reveal God's character, nature, mission, and purpose. God is present in and through the storm; not just when we are safe on the other side. We can trust that God is involved.

***

Elijah is one of the greatest prophets we read about in the Bible. You won't find a book named after him, but you'll find memorable stories of the impact he had on lives, a nation, and the world. There is a story told by Matthew, Mark, and Luke called the transfiguration.[4] It's a moment when three apostles, Peter, James, and John, encountered Jesus in a way that testified that Jesus really was God in flesh, not just a mighty prophet or simply a good human being. In that story, two men stand with Jesus: Moses and Elijah. Of all the people who could have been standing there with Jesus, Elijah was one of them.

Every Jew knew about Elijah. His memory is present at every Passover Meal, and it's not uncommon to know men who have been named after him. His name means "Yahweh is my God." His name alone is about mission.

---

[4] Matthew 17:1-8, Mark 9:2-8, and Luke 9:28-36.

Elijah was a man of God who had an impressive resume of ministry successes and powerful prophetic moments. Yet, 1 Kings 19:4 has this to say about this mighty man of faith, "But he himself went a day's journey into the wilderness, and came and sat down under a solitary broom tree. He asked that he might die: 'It is enough; now, O Lord, take away my life, for I am no better than my ancestors.'"

Even the best and the greatest can hit a wall that leaves them paralyzed in their tracks. This was one of the greatest prophets in the entire Bible, and we're told about a time he gave up hope and asked to die. Despair, worthlessness, and overwhelming anxiety can creep into the hearts of anyone.

Elijah had just come off of one of the greatest victories in the entire Bible. It was one man (Elijah), against four-hundred and fifty prophets of Baal, and Elijah won. Elijah took on hundreds in a competition to see whose God was the one, true, living God. The prophets of Baal did all they could to get their god to act, but there was nothing. Not even a peep. Elijah, displaying great confidence in his God, made sure all attention was on the moment because he knew God was about to do something amazing. And God did.

***

In between the great victory and Elijah's wish to die, he was threatened. Opposition rose up, not from King Ahab, though he had been furious with Elijah for quite some time, but from Ahab's wife, Jezebel. There's a reason we don't have friends or coworkers named Jezebel, and if you do know one, you're probably a little suspicious.

Jezebel threatened Elijah, and just like that, he was struck with fear and he fled to die.

How can one go from such an awe-inspiring victory to being in the pit of despair in the matter of hours? Isn't it wild how there can sometimes be a letdown after a peak performance or victory? We may be quick to judge Elijah as whiny or ungrateful, until we pause to see how we can easily find ourselves in this same story.

Most of us who have ever found ourselves in a pit of despair didn't ask to get in it. We didn't wish for it. We didn't plan for it. A lot of times we don't understand how it happened.

Rarely does despair knock on the door of our hearts and ask for permission. It intrudes. Despair doesn't send an email invite to go grab coffee in order to get to know each other better. It creeps into our lives in unexpected ways.

This is what happened to Elijah.

But God.

But God didn't leave him in despair.

God desired an encounter. And an encounter between God and Elijah is exactly what happened.

***

Two things I want you to notice about this story: 1) God desired an encounter with Elijah. 2) God helped prepare Elijah for the encounter.

First, God desired an encounter with Elijah.

Here's the story:

He said, "Go out and stand on the mountain before the Lord, for the Lord is about to pass by." Now there was a great wind, so strong that it was splitting mountains and breaking rocks in pieces before the Lord, but the Lord was not in the wind; and after the wind an earthquake, but the Lord was not in the earthquake; and after the earthquake a fire, but the Lord was not in the fire; and after the fire a sound of sheer silence.[5]

A great wind. A powerful storm. But God wasn't in the storm.

An earthquake. But God wasn't in the earthquake.

A fire. But God wasn't in the fire.

Then, silence. In some versions, a gentle whisper.

The Bible doesn't say that God was in the whisper, though we often assume that the Lord was. Whatever it was, the small, gentle sound convicted Elijah to the core. He was overwhelmed by the presence of God.

I wonder if God used the wind, earthquake, and fire to awaken Elijah's senses, only to capture his heart with something as small as a whisper. God wanted Elijah to know that storms surrounded him in his life and in his ministry. Storms brought challenges, opposition, hurdles, and roadblocks. Yet, through it all, God wasn't going to leave him alone. God was present in the miraculous victory over the prophets of Baal, and Elijah needed to know that God was also fully present in the small, simple moments of life too.

---

[5] 1 Kings 19:11-12.

I think God wanted to use this moment to remind Elijah of a never-ending anchor for his soul. Elijah's anchor wasn't to be based on success in ministry, miraculous events, memorable sermons, or heavenly mysteries. His anchor was in the God of the big, and the small.

Second, God helped prepare Elijah for the encounter.

Before we read this part of the story, here's what I want you to know about God: *God isn't just interested in an encounter with you, but God is in the preparation that leads to the encounter.* God isn't just at the destination. God is in the process.

After Elijah sits under a tree because he's ready to die, and before God encounters Elijah through a gentle voice, we read this:

Then he lay down under the broom tree and fell asleep. Suddenly an angel touched him and said to him, "Get up and eat." He looked, and there at his head was a cake baked on hot stones, and a jar of water. He ate and drank, and lay down again. The angel of the Lord came a second time, touched him, and said, "Get up and eat, otherwise the journey will be too much for you." He got up, and ate and drank; then he went in the strength of that food forty days and forty nights to Horeb the mount of God.[6]

In God's graciousness and generosity, the Lord sent an angel to touch Elijah's life. The Lord provided food and water, and prepared him for the journey that was ahead. Not just once. Twice. Restoring Elijah to health wasn't a simple switch God flipped, but a process of preparation. When Elijah was under the tree, he wasn't ready for an

---

[6] 1 Kings 19:5-8.

21

encounter. His senses weren't up. His heart wasn't ready. Despair had blocked his vision.

God isn't just in the encounter. God is in the preparation and the process.

***

How often do we want the encounter, but not the preparation it takes to get ready for it?

How often do we want the God of the special events, but not the God who is in the mundane, day-to-day grind of life?

How often do we want the church-camp-high, but not the daily devotion?

How often do we want a worship service to connect us to God, but we step into a worship center without having taken time to anticipate an encounter?

God doesn't prefer light-switch-spirituality. Maturity in faith is the result of dedication, preparation, and learning to trust that God is giving us food, drink, and strength for the journey.

The journey to Easter is about preparation for an encounter. We want the Easter-high, but we need the hard work of preparing our hearts for the good news that longs to fill it.

***

In January of 2020, Kayci decided she wanted to run the St. Jude half-marathon that takes place every December in Memphis. The greatest challenge in front of her for obtaining this goal was that she isn't a runner. Well, better said, she wasn't a runner.

22

Kayci joined a running group in February. Even after COVID shut many things down throughout Shelby County, she continued to run. Every Tuesday, Thursday, and Saturday, her alarm clock would go off at 4:50, and she'd run.

On the day of her race, a few friends joined me at two different locations on her half marathon to cheer her on and hold up signs:

We are proud of you.

Way to go, Kayci.

On a scale of 1-10, you're a 13.1.

There have been many moments in our marriage when I have been so proud of my wife. At the top was the delivery of our two boys. There have also been multiple speaking engagements where I have witnessed her pour hours into preparing messages to deliver, and then witnessed God work wonders.

This race wasn't at the very top, but it's definitely up there. I wasn't only proud that Kayci ran 13.1 miles on December 5, 2020, but I was proud that she put in the work for 11 months to prepare for that race. It wasn't just the experience of the race, but the process of gaining endurance so she could do it.

Prepare yourselves now for the glory that is ahead of us.

Allow God to strengthen you now, for it is through that strength that we are ready for what may come next.

May the gentle whisper slow us down enough to hear the voice of God echoing all around us reminding us that God is on the move. It is the sound that no storm can silence.

RESTING IN THE STORM

CHAPTER 3

The weekend before COVID-19 began shutting down most of the United States, I traveled to Washington D.C. to speak at an event in Fairfax. I boarded my American Airlines flight with Group 4, took my aisle seat, and waited to see if a passenger was going to take the window seat next to me. Just before the door shut, a group of college students ran onto our plane, and one young man made the motion to the window seat on my row. I stood to let him in. We proceeded to briefly introduce ourselves. He was a part of a mentoring program, and they were taking a spring break trip together.

He struggled getting his seatbelt on. He couldn't figure out how to make the two pieces click together. Before asking to assist him, I realized I was most likely sitting next to a first-time flyer. I unattached my seatbelt and walked him through how to fasten the belt. I asked if it was his first time to fly. He shook his head yes. For most of the students, they had never been on a plane before. You could tell by how big their eyes were. They were nervous, giddy, and frightened.

As we took off, my neighbor was like a small child. He elbowed me, "Man, you can see houses." Elbowed me again, "You can see cars driving on the road." Patted my leg, "Dude, you can see people playing in backyards." Then, he leaned back in his seat and put one hand on his stomach and said, "Uh-oh."

Now, if you know anything about me, my greatest phobia in life is throw up. I don't have a weak stomach, so I'm not going to throw up if you throw up. I'm just going to run for my life while having no choice but to despise the throw-up-er for the rest of my life. I must admit, I'm better at all this since becoming a dad, but still, when a hand goes to the stomach and someone says, "Uh-oh," my first inclination is to punch them in the face, grab a parachute, and jump.

This time, I jumped into action in a different way. I pointed to the paper bag in the seat pocket in front of him, and then said, "Bro, this ain't happening. Not on my watch. Not today."

I patted his leg, "Look at me! Look at me!" He glanced over toward me.

I said, "Breathe. Lean back. Take a breath."

I did it with him. Together, we took a few deep breaths. And my friend was good for the remainder of the flight.

You want to know what was ironic? I traveled to Fairfax to speak at an event in which the theme was, "Breathe!" I felt really good about the content I carried with me into the event. David Fraze, a good friend of mine and well-known speaker, and I were speaking four times from Ezekiel 37. It's a vision the Lord gives the prophet, Ezekiel, and *breathing* is a significant part of the story.

In the vision, there are bodies that look like they're alive, but they're not, because there is no breath in them. Preparing to speak on this specific topic was challenging for my own soul because often my pace in life isn't conducive to taking good, long, healthy breaths. I'm addicted to adrenaline. I love speed. I like to clip along at a fast pace. I struggle to understand why people don't want to move at my pace, but then I'm given feedback on how I make people feel extremely tired, because my pace in life isn't sustainable. It doesn't need to be repeated or mimicked. There is no telling how many times a day God is trying to get my attention by saying, "Breathe! Please, Josh! Take a breath. Slow down enough to catch your breath. Look at me! Breathe!"

I traveled back to Memphis where within five days, nearly everything in our country was shut down. Schools shut down. Churches suspended in-person gatherings. Restaurants pivoted to carry out or delivery only.

Over the next few days, I jumped on FaceTime with members at Sycamore View who were paralyzed with anxiety, fear, and paranoia. My message in my sermons and in pastoral interactions became the same message as the one I gave to the young man sitting next to me on the plane, "Look at me. Breathe! Take a breath. Center yourself in God."

***

There's no one who models this better than Jesus.

Shortly after Matthew gives us the Sermon on the Mount, Jesus and His disciples got into a boat. All of the sudden a windstorm arose, and we're told, "The waves swept over the boat."[7]

The irony in Matthew's story is that the boat is getting battered by the waves, but Jesus is sound asleep. Maybe the energy Jesus had poured into preaching, healing, and discipling had finally gotten the best of Him. Maybe it was a Sunday afternoon and Jesus modeled what a good Sunday afternoon nap was supposed to be like. All we

---

[7] Matthew 8:24.

know is that the disciples are freaking out thinking they're about to die, and Jesus is in the fetal position sleeping like a baby.

The rest of the story goes like this:
The disciples went and woke him, saying, "Lord, save us! We're going to drown!" He replied, "You of little faith, why are you so afraid?" Then he got up and rebuked the winds and the waves, and it was completely calm. The men were amazed and asked, "What kind of man is this? Even the winds and the waves obey him!"[8]

Notice how the story unfolds: They wake Jesus up. Jesus converses with the disciples. Then, Jesus rebukes the wind, which is the same word used to describe how Jesus drove out demons.[9] Jesus uses energy and emotion to set wrongs right. Last but not least, when all things are made right, there is acknowledgement that the power of God has been displayed for them to see.

In chapter 8, Matthew is in the middle of telling stories in order to declare that Jesus is Lord over everything. In chapters 8 and 9, he strings together stories announcing that Jesus is Lord over physical diseases, social diseases, paralysis, fever, evil, demon possession, death, loss of sight, loss of the ability to speak, and yes, nature. There's nothing Jesus isn't Lord over. He is Lord over everything.

However, how was Jesus able to rest so well, and so easily, while in the storm?

***

---

[8] Matthew 8:25-27.

[9] It is the Greek word "ἐπετίμησεν," which means to express strong disapproval of someone. It is to rebuke, reprove, or censure.

When our family hunkered down during Hurricane Sally, our phones began blowing up around midnight. We were being told that we were under a tornado warning. If you don't know the difference between a tornado warning and a tornado watch, a watch means that you need to be prepared. A warning means you need to take action immediately.

If we were in our home in Memphis, we would have gone to the closet, but what do you do when you're on the 16th floor? We decided to go to the bathroom in the center of the condo. We picked up blankets and pillows and sprang into action.

Well, three of us did; Truitt was sound asleep. I woke him up saying, "Truitt, there's a tornado outside. We've got to move to the bathroom right now." He slowly walked to the bathroom, laid down on the tile floor, covered up with his blanket, and fell asleep. I have it on video.

How was he able to sleep that hard during a hurricane and a tornado warning? We joked with him for the next few days that he was like Jesus on the boat getting rest in the storm.

Is it possible? Resting in a storm? Can we really do it?

I think the answer is that rest comes easier to those who are properly anchored. But that's easier said than done, right?

***

When we move through the storms of life, it can cause us to forget to do the simple things. This is why when people walk through divorce, miscarriages, the loss of a job, or the death of a loved one, people have to remind us to eat, get dressed, take a shower, and to do the simple things. For anyone battling forms of anxiety, depression, or stress, rest doesn't come easy. The reality is we are off a little bit.

A couple of months into our journey through COVID-19, I brought in a well-respected psychologist to talk with our ministry staff at Sycamore View. She said that some psychologists argue that a crisis lasts about six weeks. After that, people deal with chronic stress. They also say that as we navigate crisis and chronic stress, we function at about 60-80% capacity.

Think about it, COVID enough could do us in, but then add onto that social unrest, racial inequality, a heated presidential election, and all the emotions going into masks, protocols, and guidelines, and our entire society is walking on eggshells.

How do we rest when there is so much work to be done?

How do we rest when there are so many people to love?

How do we rest when so much of cable news is telling us there are so many people to hate? After all, hating other people and groups takes a lot of energy.

How do we rest when there are agendas to tackle?

How do we rest when there are tasks to accomplish?

How do we rest when anxiety and stress just won't leave us alone?

Let's be honest, *resting* often doesn't feel productive.

No rest for the weary works well for parents with newborns in the home.

No rest for the weary works for healthcare workers dealing with pandemics.

No rest for the weary works for some jobs, some family situations, and some seasons of life.

Yet, no rest for the weary isn't a rhythm of life the Bible promotes or suggests.

A rest-less life isn't a rhythm you find in Jesus.

It's not how God desires for us to live.

There are two times Jesus declares that all authority and all things have been handed over to Him.

One of those occasions is in the Great Commission found in Matthew 28, "All authority in heaven and on earth has been given to me."[10]

The other time is found in Matthew 11, "*All things* have been handed over to me by my Father."[11]

In the Great Commission, Jesus accepts the authority, and then uses it to commission people to be about His work in the world.

In Matthew 11, Jesus receives that authority, and here's what He does with it, "Come to me, all you that are weary and are carrying heavy burdens, and I will give you rest. Take my yoke upon you, and

---

[10] Matthew 28:18.

[11] Matthew 11:27.

learn from me; for I am gentle and humble in heart, and you will find rest for your souls. For my yoke is easy, and my burden is light."[12]

With authority, Jesus invites people into rest.

***

Every moment we are alive, there are close to two thousand thunderstorms happening throughout the world. It may be nothing but sunshine where you are, but there's a storm brewing somewhere.

In life, there will always be storms around us. Some that we find ourselves in, and others that are hammering the people around us.

Anchoring our faith in Jesus is the best way to assure a healthy rhythm and rest in life. Anchoring in Jesus doesn't mean we will live storm-less lives, but that we will have assurance that there is a connection with God and with others that will survive the waves.

This assurance doesn't alleviate anxiety or stress, but it can give us rest in the storm. Some may call it—a peace that transcends all understanding.

***

I don't know exactly how God is going to help you as you navigate your own storms. I don't know how God desires to reveal the love and power of Jesus to your heart. I simply choose to believe that God is eager to refine our character, to protect our joy, and to teach us how to remain faithful witnesses to Jesus no matter what.

---

[12] Matthew 11:28-30.

So, let's breathe.

Lean back.

Take a breath.

Open your ears.

Let God speak into your heart.

WALKING OVER THE STORM

CHAPTER 4

In the summer of 2019, we took a trip of a lifetime and traveled all the way out to the west coast. Over sixteen days, we put 5700 miles on our van. We spent time at Carlsbad Caverns, Disneyland, Universal Studios, the Hoover Dam, and two different locations at the Grand Canyon.

We also stopped at four baseball stadiums. Every year since 2012, I have taken my boys on a dad/son baseball trip. Our goal is to make it to every ballpark by the time they graduate high school. It has been a fun way to see the country. On our road trip, we saw the Diamondbacks, Dodgers, Angels, and Padres.

Kayci doesn't go to baseball stadiums with us, but she was pretty adamant about going to a Dodger's game. It's not that she's a big Dodger's fan, but that she wanted to eat a Dodger Dog in Dodger's Stadium.

In San Diego, our hotel was downtown, which is where the Padres stadium is located. The boys and I went to the game, while Kayci stayed back in the hotel to watch Hallmark and enjoy some peace and quiet.

Towards the end of the game, Kayci texted me that she found a restaurant a couple of blocks from the stadium, that she was on the patio, and to meet her after the game. So, when the boys and I left, we went to meet up with Kayci.

I had already eaten at the game, but the moment I peeked at the menu, I noticed Jambalaya. We all have foods that make us hungry even when we think we're not hungry. Jambalaya is one of those for me, so I ordered it. Shortly after placing my order, my boys began nagging each other. I think they were ready to get back to the room to play electronics and swim. Kids are smart and I think they know that if they agitate each other enough, the parents will hurry through certain activities to get them home. I asked for the ticket, paid for our meal, finished my dinner, and we left.

The next morning, I woke up before the family and went to the gym. On the way to enjoy my morning workout, I noticed a gift shop. Kayci enjoys collecting salt and pepper shakers, so I decided to buy her one. I stepped up to the cashier, reached for my money clip to pull out the credit card, and it wasn't there. I had left it in at the restaurant the night before. Immediately, I blamed it on the boys, then I called the restaurant. Thankfully, they said there were seven credit cards left there the night before. Unfortunately, none of them were mine. I called and cancelled our card. Thankfully, we had another one to use to help get us home.

In my hotel room was a book I had been devouring by Ruth Haley Barton, *Strengthening the Soul of Your Leadership*. In the introduction of her book, she says that losing your soul is often like using your credit card. You don't know you've lost it, until you reach for it, and it's not there. I remember reading that and thinking to myself, "Great metaphor. So powerful. Even though I don't lose credit cards or keys, I get it." I take great pride in not losing things like that, yet there I was in San Diego having lost a credit card.

2019 was a rough year for my morale and confidence. I have a great ministry at Sycamore View, but there were a few challenges from 2019 that got the best of me. Barton's book was healing for my soul. Her point about losing credit cards and losing one's soul wasn't about losing salvation, but one's anchor. There in San Diego, God and I had a good, long talk. It was like God was saying, "Josh, you're off a little bit. There's some work I need to do with you. I think I have your attention now. Let's get to work. There are a few things I have to teach you."

***

As we navigate the storms of life, there is a God who walks with us, and that same God is eager to teach us valuable lessons about His heart, mission, character, and nature.

As we travel down painful roads, the last thing we may want to think about is pulling up a chair, taking out a pen and a pad, and leaning in to take notes from a teacher.

Yet, whether it is COVID, death, or relational dysfunction, God is eager to equip Jesus's church to faithfully walk-through life as ambassadors for hope. God teaches through storms, yet, students have to be prepared and willing to learn. I don't think it's that God takes us to school by causing us to suffer, but that God makes the most of teachable moments in order to refine character.

As God teaches, we may not get an answer to the *why*, but God diligently works to equip us for the *how*. Answering the *why* isn't God's primary agenda. Teaching us *how* to be faithful no matter what storms come in life is the work of the Kingdom of God. I don't believe God is behind every form of pain we experience in life, but I do believe that God can use whatever pain comes our way to teach our hearts about courage, joy, hope, adventure, and faithfulness.

***

Matthew 8 isn't the only story told about Jesus and storms. A few chapters later, we find Jesus in a storm again. This time, Jesus had just been handed the news that John the Baptist had been murdered at the hands of Herod. In deep distress, Jesus attempted to get away from the crowd to be alone. I imagine Jesus wanting some space to mourn, grieve, and process life. There was the terrible news of his relative John being beheaded, but there was also the reality that what happened to John, in a way, was going to happen to Him too.

As Jesus withdrew, the crowds kept coming. The next thing we witness is Jesus feeding thousands of people. Think about it: in Jesus' sadness, grief, and sorrow, He performs one of the greatest miracles told in the gospels. In fact, outside of the miracle of the resurrection of Jesus, it's the only miracle told in all four gospels. Just like Jesus, some of the best ministry that may flow from our lives flows when we are in dark places.

After stuffing bellies with fish and bread, we're told, "Jesus made the disciples get into the boat."[13] I'm sure there were disciples saying, "Jesus, we don't do boats," or, "Jesus, give me a couple hours. I'm stuffed." But the command had been given, "Get in the boat!"

As the boat left shore, Jesus went up on a mountain to pray. Much like Matthew 8, a storm came upon the sea and the boat was being battered by the waves.

I've been to the Sea of Galilee, and I have witnessed how quickly a storm can come upon the sea. It doesn't take long for the sea to go from perfectly calm to battering waves.

[13] Matthew 14:22.

Interestingly, the disciples struggled for over six hours while Jesus stayed on the mountain praying. Most likely, Jesus could see that a storm had come upon the sea where His disciples sailed, yet Jesus chose to remain in the place of prayer until He felt released from the time He needed with God.

Early in the morning, Jesus began walking toward them on the water. In Mark's gospel, he writes, "Walking on the lake, He was about to pass them by..."[14] It's like Jesus was just taking a stroll.

However, in Matthew's gospel, a conversation ensued. The disciples think it's a ghost. When you're in the middle of a storm, it's hard to see straight; it's also hard to think straight. Jesus responded by saying, "Take courage. It is I. Don't be afraid."[15]

The next few verses are described like this: *"Lord, if it's you," Peter replied, "tell me to come to you on the water." "Come," Jesus said. Then Peter got down out of the boat, walked on the water and came toward Jesus. But when he saw the wind, he was afraid and, beginning to sink, cried out, "Lord, save me!" Immediately Jesus reached out his hand and caught him. "You of little faith," he said, "why did you doubt?"[16]*

I'm struck by what happens next. "When they climbed into the boat, the wind died down."[17] The wind and waves didn't stop until Jesus and Peter were back in the boat. Jesus could have calmed the

---

[14] Mark 6:48.

[15] Matthew 14:27.

[16] Matthew 14:28-31.

[17] Matthew 14:32.

storm before getting back to the boat. It would have made their journey back to the boat easier. I think Jesus wanted to teach Peter that with Jesus, we can conquer and navigate our way over and through the storms of life.

The disciples responded by worshipping Jesus, "Truly you are the Son of God."[18]

***

In life, rarely do we go looking for storms. The storms of life find us. We don't intentionally drive into the eye of a thunderstorm, tornado, hurricane, or flood. But each one of these will come upon us, most likely, in seasons when we least expect it. One day, the sky looks clear, and the next thing we know, we're in a storm and we can't find our way out.

I want to give you a few equipping pieces based on the two storms Jesus faced in his life. I hope this will comfort you in your storm, or that a nugget of wisdom will equip you for when the storms of life come.

First, the One who conquered the storm is the One who could have held back the storm. If Jesus had the power to make the storm stop, you'd think He'd also have the power to keep the storm from coming in the first place. This has baffled people and has caused all kinds of faith struggles over the years. Why does God allow storms? Why does God allow suffering to happen? God has the power to hold it back, so why?

---

[18] Matthew 14:33.

I've come to believe that Jesus did not come to heal the world of disease, but to launch a movement that would transform the world. Until Jesus returns to set all things right, storms will remain a part of life as we know it. We don't ask for them, but they are part of the world we are born into. God does not orchestrate every storm, but God can prepare us to navigate it. God isn't the creator of every painful encounter that comes our way, but God is the sustainer of the weak, redeemer of the broken, and comforter for the afflicted.

Second, Jesus slept through one storm, and walked through the other. This isn't to say that Jesus didn't take storms seriously. However, there was a non-anxious presence about Jesus. He modeled how there can truly be a peace that transcends all understanding. Jesus was able to put the storms of life in their proper place. He knew they didn't get the last word. He knew they wouldn't last forever. He knew they wouldn't win. For Jesus, He refused to allow storms to define His identity or to have power over His life.

Third, everything Jesus spoke was in the midst of the storm. In the two stories Matthew tells about Jesus and storms, if you have the red letters in your Bible, Jesus only spoke while the waves were battering the boat. In Matthew 8, Jesus asks a question about their faith. In Matthew 14, He assured them of who He was, and He conversed with Peter.

If you've ever tried to talk to someone while standing in a storm, it can be hard to hear each other. You have to yell in effort to communicate. As we travel through grief, pain, and even COVID, know that Jesus is diligently attempting to teach us while in the storm. Jesus doesn't wait until we get to the other side of painful events to sit us down and share wisdom with us; instead, Jesus speaks to us while we are navigating brokenness. For those of you currently engaged in the storms of life, listen for the red letters and the voice of God.

Fourth, Jesus spoke directly to fear. Jesus doesn't want anyone to be taken down by unhealthy forms of anxiety, paranoia, or fear. As Jesus spoke during both storms, He addressed fear. He called His disciples to radical faith even when things seemed to be utterly out of control.

I can't help but imagine the power of these two stories in the lives of the disciples, especially Peter. I wonder how many times Jesus-followers found themselves in prisons, jail cells, and hunted by persecutors, yet they remembered that God had walked with them over and through the storms of life before, and that God would do it again.

I wonder if Peter would have had the courage, bravery, and audacity to preach the way he did in the book of Acts if Jesus hadn't walked with him over the storms before.

Jesus doesn't deny that fear exists. I think Jesus acknowledges that there are a lot of reasons to be afraid. Yet, Jesus never wants to see His people taken down by fear. The mission of God is never put on hold or set aside. He continues through all seasons.

Fifth, storms will pass. Storms are temporary. They will not last forever. Though there are times we wonder where the finish line is with COVID, suffering, or pain, we know that storms will pass.

Unfortunately, we also know that storms can leave a path of destruction behind them, and that life may not return to what it used to be. Our hope is in a God who will not let the destruction caused by storms get the last word.

Finally, our God will be worshipped. Both stories of Jesus navigating storms end with praise, honor, and recognition that God is fully alive and at work in the world. The disciples know that Jesus did the impossible. We can bank on the same too. God's not going to let storms get the last word.

As we walk through pain, I think one of the healthiest things we can do is pray, "God, I believe that you are bigger than this pain I feel. I believe that you will not leave me alone. I believe that you can use this season I am in to refine my character and to mold my heart. Do not let this season rob me of joy, adventure, or courage. Speak to me God, your servant is listening."

***

As I said earlier, I hit a low spot in 2019. My morale and confidence took a major hit. It wasn't just one event that nearly did me in, but a combination of multiple events that collided in my life all at the same time.

I had a few friends who stepped up in my life to remind me of my calling. In many ways, they became the voice of God for me.

I began seeing my therapist more regularly. Dr. Katherine Blackney has been a gift of God in my life. She's a therapist who knows how to listen well, but she is also willing to ask hard questions that force me to process my pain.

As God often does, God also used the most unlikely people and the most unexpected moments to speak words of truth into my heart.

In September of 2019, I went to visit a friend of mine, Pat Simon, who was in hospice care. She had been given a few days to live. Pat had a remarkable story. For many years of her life, she was an angry woman, but in the last ten years of her life, God renovated and reshaped her heart. She was a woman full of the Holy Spirit. The joy of the Lord permeated all around her. She had the gift of encouragement. Everywhere she went, people received a touch of God through her life.

I sat down next to Pat. Her arms were swollen, she struggled to breathe, yet she smiled and reached to hold my hand.

She asked me about heaven. We talked about it for a few minutes. She shared with me again about how God had transformed her life.

We prayed together. I kissed her on the forehead, and I told her how much I loved her.

As I walked out of the room, Pat said, "Wait, Josh. I feel like God has given me a word to speak to you. Come back over here and sit down."

I had somewhere to be. I was scheduled to speak at a chapel service at the Harding School of Theology. However, if a dying woman tells you to sit down because she has a word of the Lord for you, you sit down!

She took my hand, and she said, "Josh, you have a tender heart. And tender hearts break easy. I bet your heart has been broken this year. God wants you to know that having a tender heart is a gift. It's a good thing. God wants you to know that whenever your heart breaks, God's not going to leave you broken. God will repair your heart. But right now, God wants you to know that having a tender heart is a gift."

A few minutes later when I got to the car, I sat there and wept.

***

One thing I know is that if we want to learn in life, we have to be willing and prepared to be taught. Students have to wake up ready to receive from their teacher.

The storms of life have so much to teach us about faithfulness, character, integrity, loyalty, and passion. In storms, know that Jesus often becomes an incredible teacher.

The journey to Easter is a journey of riding the waves of life. It's a journey of stripping off everything that hinders, and allowing our character to be refined by God.

It's a journey.

It's a season.

If you feel lost, this is a season that is designed to help you find your way again.

Anchors can be reestablished in our lives.

God has so much to teach you, to give you, to extend to you.

Open your ears, eyes, and heart.

Receive.

Listen.

Be taught.

Be renewed.

OBEYING IN THE STORM

CHAPTER 5

Kayci and I have two boys. Our oldest is Joshua Truitt. He goes by Truitt. When we decided on his name, we had only heard of a few Truitts before, and the three we had heard of went with an "e" instead of an "i." There is Truett Seminary at Baylor, but I can honestly say that had no bearing on naming him Truitt. Then, there is Samuel Truett Cathy, the founder of Chick-fil-A. Yet, the one that really caught our attention was Toby Mac's son, Truett. I have been a huge fan of Toby since his DC Talk days, and the bond he had with his son, Truett, was inspiring. The name Truitt means honesty, trustfulness. We fell in love with the name.

Our youngest son is Noah James. His middle name was chosen because the book of James is one of Kayci's favorite books in the Bible. It's a tie between James and Ephesians. We thought Noah would appreciate us going with *Noah James* instead of *Noah Ephesians*. Noah is a name we agreed on early in her pregnancy. No, it's not because *The Notebook* is our favorite movie. It's because Kayci loves the character Noah in the Bible.

Here is what Genesis 5:29 has to say about Noah's birth, "[Lamech] named him Noah, saying, 'Out of the ground that the Lord has cursed this one shall bring us relief from our work and from the toil of our hands.'" At birth, there was a calling, mission, and expectation placed on his life.

However, the verse that drew us in was Genesis 6:9, "Noah was a righteous man, blameless in his generation; Noah walked with God." Righteous. Blameless. Walked with God. What else does a parent want for their children?

***

When we chose to name our youngest son, Noah, we knew we were choosing a character whose story was complicated. There's a VBS version of Noah, and then there's the non-watered-down version. It's a story with problems, consequences, punishment, destruction, salvation, and promises.

It's one of the most well-known storms in the entire Bible. It rained non-stop for weeks. The storm caused a lot of destruction. Countless lives were lost. It's not just the most remembered storm in the Bible, but even non-Christians and non-Jews reference the story today. If people hear someone say, "It's raining so hard today, someone needs to build an ark," most people know what story is being referenced.

I'm most interested in what the story tells us about God. I think one of the best and healthiest ways to reflect on stories like this is to look to see how other voices throughout the Bible talk about the story. Is it a story that is used to shape and form generation after generation? If so, how? And well, the Bible spends very little time talking about Noah. As much as it's a go-to Bible story for kids, it's not a go-to story throughout the Bible. Isaiah and Ezekiel make brief references to Noah, but that's about it in the Old Testament. The story of Noah doesn't get much playing time in the New Testament either, but Jesus, Hebrews, and Peter use Noah to teach, encourage, warn, and inspire. But before we look at New Testament voices, let's look at the story.

***

God was very specific with Noah about why the world needed to be purified. Evil and violence had gotten out of hand. We aren't given a lot of details, we're just told that violence was everywhere.[19] God created the earth and humanity with harmony in mind, not destruction. Violence doesn't advance the mission of God, and violence rarely leads to unity and peace. I think that's why this story is so hard for some people to wrap their minds around. It sure does sound like God uses violence because God is frustrated with violence.

I think a better way to think about this is God has always been deeply concerned about setting the world right. There are times when God has had to purify hearts, nations, and the world. I can't grasp that God is ever driven by a joyful desire to destroy. I can grasp that God is eager to purify the world of destructive behavior and practices. It breaks God's heart to see evil spread like wildfire. It hurts heaven to see righteousness blatantly disregarded.

God purifying the world by sending a deadly flood is part of the Bible. This isn't a defining characteristic of the nature of God seen throughout Scripture. It's a story we have to wrestle with, but not a story meant to become how we know God. I think this is important, because as we attempt to anchor in our own storms, we can easily wonder what God is up to. For me, I want to teach people to come to the Bible this way: *if you want to know what God is like, look at Jesus.*

***

With that in mind, here are two threads that we see in the Noah narrative that also play out throughout the pages of the Bible: 1) God uses people, and 2) God asks for radical obedience.

---

[19] Genesis 6:11.

First, *God uses people.* God has a long track record of using people to accomplish heavenly assignments. God could have purified the world in a number of different ways, yet God decided that the process of having a few humans build an ark was the way to go. God chose to preserve the world, and to purify the world, through human collaboration. There are times today when we look at God and say, "You go, God. Go save the world. Heal the world. Redeem the world. We're asking you to do this. We are cheering for you to do this." And God's response is, "I'm working to save and heal the world, and who's coming with me?" God isn't looking for permission to accomplish heavenly assignments, but God is looking for collaboration and cooperation.

Second, *God asks for radical obedience.* Even if, like Noah, you look like a complete fool in the eyes of the world, obedience matters to heaven. We don't know if boats were even a thing prior to Noah. Yet, God gave instructions and Noah went for it. Noah doesn't argue with God. Noah doesn't even argue for certain animals. I mean, come on, there are some animals we would have asked God to not let on the ark, "God, do we really need squirrels, mambas, and poodles?" Yet, there was no bargaining. No complaining. No questioning.

***

Jesus references the Noah story in Matthew 24:36-39 when He talks about the coming of the Son of Man. Noah finds his way into Hebrews' Hall of Fame of Faith, "By faith *Noah*, warned by God about events as yet unseen, respected the warning and built an ark to save his household; by this he condemned the world and became an heir to the righteousness that is in accordance with faith."[20]

---

[20] Hebrews 11:7.

49

Peter is the only other New Testament writer to give voice to Noah, and I think the way Peter uses the Noah narrative is significant. Peter most likely wrote his first letter to rural churches who were facing social pressure. Though there may have been some physical persecution that occasionally took place in these areas, the greater impact was social pressure which would have led to both relational and economic hardships.

If you became a follower of Jesus in the churches Peter wrote to, there's a good chance you had either left paganism or Judaism to become a Jesus-follower. Commitment to Christ meant that there were certain events, practices, and ways of life that one no longer participated in. For many of us who became Jesus-followers while living in the United States, our conversions were followed by joy, excitement, and other forms of congratulations. However, in many parts of the world, the decision to follow Jesus means severed relationships, loss of job, and other significant economic and social consequences.

Peter wrote to encourage the church in their faith. He wrote to anchor them in the Jesus-story. Suffering, hardship, and pain are parts of all of our stories. If we are anchored in to the wrong things, we drift. Peter was deeply concerned about faithfulness even as the storms of life raged.

It's with this context that Peter writes, "God waited patiently in the days of Noah, during the building of the ark, in which a few, that is, eight persons, were saved through water. And baptism, which this prefigured, now saves you—not as a removal of dirt from the body, but as an appeal to God for a good conscience, through the resurrection of Jesus Christ, who has gone into heaven and is at the right hand of God, with angels, authorities, and powers made subject to him."[21]

Peter had most likely been in two different storms with Jesus. We assume he was in the boat when Jesus slept through one storm, and we know he was in the boat when Jesus walked over the water. Peter had been through storms with Jesus and it had changed him forever.

Peter knew there were people scattered all over Asia Minor who found themselves in different types of storms. Therefore, Peter took a page from one of the most memorable stories in the Bible and used it to encourage the people in their faith. Specifically, Peter used the Noah story to remind people of God's patience, God's salvation, and how their baptisms are an appeal to God for a good conscience.

For Peter's audience, and for us, the storms of life can mess with our morale, confidence, and self-worth. They can conjure up memories of the past. They can mess with our minds. Peter affirms that through Jesus we have a clean, clear conscience. This serves as an anchor for the soul.

It's kind of odd, isn't it? Noah's story that messes with our conscience because it wipes out so much of life, is the same story Peter uses to appeal to having a clear conscience. Peter appeals to the Noah story through the Jesus story.

Through the storms of life, know this, we can anchor in these truths:

God uses people.
God asks for obedience.
God gifts clear consciences.

---

[21] 1 Peter 3:20-22.

SWALLOWED BY THE STORM

CHAPTER 6

Kayci and I take a trip every year with no kids. It has been a discipline of ours since our oldest was born. Sometimes people ask how we can go a week without seeing our kids. Our response is, well, it's really not that hard. We slow down our van when we pull up to their grandparents's home, we toss the luggage out the sliding door, the boys jump out, and we speed away.

In the fall of 2019, we boarded a cruise ship in New York City and traveled up the northeastern coast porting at a few places along the way. It's called a fall foliage cruise. Kayci loves to witness leaves changing colors in the fall, and this cruise is perfect for people who share that passion. We traveled with some of our best friends, Todd and Krista. It was a seven-day cruise, and the first six days were full of tours, walks, bike rides, coffee shops, museums, and beauty. The final day of our cruise was a sea day to travel back to New York City. And that is when things got interesting.

The captain had been following a tropical storm that had made its way up the coast. He warned that our sea day was going to be a rough ride. He didn't hold anything back. In fact, he went as far to say that they were giving away free motion sickness medicine at guest services for anyone who needed some. For over twelve hours, we traveled through twenty-five-foot waves toward our destination. Water was splashing all the way up to the 4th and 5th levels of the boat. We survived. We will cruise again at some point. You may read this chapter and decide to never cruise again. If so, I'm sorry.

Storms don't ask for permission. They form, travel, and do their thing. This is true with tropical storms, thunderstorms, and wind. It's also true with the storms that come in life in the form of cancer, heartache, depression, and chronic stress.

***

Two of the most told stories in the entire Bible involve storms: Noah and Jonah. I'm pretty sure whoever created the idea behind Vacation Bible School (VBS) wrote into the VBS by-laws that Noah and Jonah had to be mainstays. They are two stories that non-Christians and non-Jews are familiar with. As popular as these two stories are, it's somewhat odd that they're barely mentioned in the New Testament.

Jonah's name means "dove." We know very little about him. We don't know if he was a well-seasoned prophet. 2 Kings 14:25 references him as a servant and prophet, but outside of that, we don't have much. We don't know anything about his family. We don't know how old he was when this story took place.

It's a bizarre story. So bizarre, it's hard to believe. Yet, at the same time, there is so much to glean from its content.

Here's the gist of the story: God told Jonah to go preach in a city called Nineveh. This was a mission trip. This was outside of Jonah's territory. He had no connections there. Sometimes God sends us to places where we've never been before. God was very specific as for the content that needed to be communicated. It wasn't grace, love, and mercy. It was a harsh rebuke for Nineveh's rebellion and unfaithfulness.

Nineveh wasn't just any city. It was the capital of Assyria and one of the most powerful cities in the world. We are told that the city was so large, it was a three-days walk from one side to the other.

Everyone around knew about the reputation of the Assyrian military. They were a force to be reckoned with. To go preach against them must have sounded like a death sentence. I know this as a preacher myself, preachers like to preach where they feel like they will be well received, not crucified. For me, I've stepped into places before where I knew my message may not be well received, but I also knew that the negative responses would probably come in the form of arguments, anonymous letters, or passive-aggressive social media posts. I didn't fear for my life.

Jonah doesn't just ignore the command of God. He gets on a boat and goes in the opposite direction. Jonah didn't appreciate the assignment God handed down to him. Jonah wasn't against prophesying, he just preferred to do it on his terms. But this isn't how things work in the Kingdom of God.

There are consequences to all forms of rebellion and disobedience. God's punishment isn't for punishment's sake alone, but because God wants to set all things right. A mighty storm came over the ship, and Jonah knew exactly what was happening. Jonah ran from a mission, rebelled against God's mission, but even more than the mission, against God alone.

Jonah's anchor had failed him. He wasn't properly anchored. When ministry didn't fit his schedule, his plan, and his expectations, he jumped ship. Everyone on the boat thought they were going to die. Yet, after a conversation with the men on the ship, Jonah talked them into throwing him overboard. They did. And he's swallowed by a fish. That's where Jonah lived for three days and three nights.

Living in the belly of fish is a big part of this story of Jonah, but there is so much more going on than Jonah and a whale. This is a narrative about God and God's heart. In the story of Jonah, God used a storm to wake Jonah up to a mission, because God was eager to dispense grace upon a city that was known for so much evil. This is the God we serve.

The book of Jonah is about:

- God displaying love and kindness to an evil city.
- God willingly choosing to use human beings to accomplish Kingdom agendas.
- God being exactly who God says He is.

Jonah ended up going to Nineveh, preaching a message, and the people responded. Jonah 4:5 says, "The people of Nineveh believed God; they proclaimed a fast, and everyone, great and small, put on sackcloth." The mercy of God fell upon a city and there was an awakening.

Unfortunately, Jonah didn't like God's response to Nineveh. God wanted Jonah to believe that Ninevites' lives mattered, and Jonah didn't want any of it. Jonah was ticked that God did what God does. Jonah 4:2, "He prayed to the Lord and said, 'O Lord! Is not this what I said while I was still in my own country? That is why I fled to Tarshish at the beginning; *for I knew that you are a gracious God and merciful, slow to anger, and abounding in steadfast love, and ready to relent from punishment*."

Jonah quoted from Exodus 34:6. The Old Testament quotes from Exodus 34:5-7 more than any other place in the Bible. God declares what God's heart is like, and it's echoed throughout Scripture. Jonah knew this truth, and then got mad that God lived up to it. Jonah wanted people to die. God wants people to live.

***

Jesus is the only one who references Jonah in the entire New Testament. It's a children's ministry favorite, yet the New Testament gives it very little playing time. However, the fact that Jesus references it as if people knew the story means it had formed people over time. Jesus assumed people knew about Jonah.

Jesus takes one of the worst storms in the entire Bible and uses it to talk about his own death, burial, and resurrection. Jonah ran from the mission of God. Jesus was talking to people who were refusing to believe the mission of God. Even though Jesus was tasked by God to die the death of crucifixion, He refused to run in the opposite direction.

Jesus is everything Jonah is not. Jesus wants people to be redeemed. Jesus wants to partner with people to advance God's purposes in the world. Everything we see Jesus say and do is a reflection of exactly who God has been all along.

To anchor in faith isn't to stay still and tread water. It is to be on mission. It isn't to play it safe. It is to go where God is eager to work in the world. In whatever storms life brings at you, you don't have to be directionless. The storm isn't the mission. The mission will always outlive the storm.

***

The story of Jonah is told in four, short chapters. It ends as a cliffhanger.

The last statement in the book is God talking to Jonah, and here's what God says, "And should I not be concerned about Nineveh, that great city, in which there are more than a hundred and twenty thousand persons who do not know their right hand from their left, and also many animals?"[22]

And that's it. That's how the story ends.

It ends with, "And also many animals?"

What kind of ending is that?

It's odd.

It's also open-ended.

And that is what is so brilliant about how the book ends. I think it's a literary move. The story has been told. But you aren't told exactly how the story ends. It's because the story of Jonah is in all of us. And we get to join God in how this story is going to play itself out.

This kind of ending isn't unique to the Bible.

The story of the prodigal son in Luke 15 ends with a dad standing with the older son outside the party because the oldest son is upset that the younger son is having a party thrown for him. Does the father and older son end up going into the party or not? It ends with them standing there. We've all been the younger brother and the older brother. What's it going to be? Are we going to join in the celebration, or stay outside?

The book of Acts ends open-ended. Paul makes it to Rome and lives there for two years. And that's it. It ends with a dot...dot...dot...as if to say, "We all get to live out the rest of the book of Acts." The story is still unfolding.

---

22 Jonah 4:11.

Through rebellion, disobedience, and the struggle to understand God's mercy, we still have a chance to join (and re-join) God's mission. There is a place for you in the unfolding story of God. No storm can keep you from it.

EATING AND DRINKING IN THE STORM

CHAPTER 7

When the Sycamore View Church first decided to suspend in-person worship services in March 2020 due to COVID-19, I was sitting at Soul Fish Cafe with three close friends: Chris Altrock, David Jordan, and Jerry Taylor. As we ate fish, fried okra, and hushpuppies, we discussed many different topics. I don't think any of us knew that as we left Soul Fish, dining in restaurants and eating meals with friends was about to change for the foreseeable future.

I'm writing this book in January of 2020. For nearly a year, our weekly staff lunch after our Monday meetings hasn't happened. Date nights have been altered. A few guy's nights have happened, but not as frequent as they did pre-pandemic.

But there is a meal I have missed more than any of these.

I miss a lot of things about not having a larger crowd together for our in-person worship services. I miss the singing, the feedback as I preach, and seeing peoples' faces as we pursue God together. Yet, the Lord's Table is what I miss the most. We still regularly celebrate the bread and cup, but it's not the same without a room full of people from all different walks of life who share in the one meal that will hold us together throughout eternity. It's the meal that brings together rich and poor, white, black, and brown, Republicans and Democrats, old and young, dog-lovers and cat-lovers, suburban, urban, and rural. It's a moment of connection, unity, and mission. And I miss it.

There are a few meals that we read about throughout the Bible. Jesus ate at least eight meals in the gospel of Luke. You can read about tables in the lives of Abraham, Jacob, Joseph, Moses, David, Paul and the church throughout the book of Acts.

Yet, there is one meal that happens during a storm. Who eats during a storm, right? But it happens, and how it happens is inspiring.

Hang on tight. We'll get to this story in just a few moments. First, a different story.

***

For New Years in 2006, Kayci and I traveled to the Bay Area for a few days. Kayci was five months pregnant with our first child. We spent a few days in San Francisco, and then rented a car to drive to Yosemite for three days. We had rented a condo at the very top of Yosemite. What better way to ring in the new year, right?

The drive through the mountains was absolutely gorgeous. We drove next to a running stream for quite some time. This wasn't what we were used to living in Texas. We had picked out a few spots we wanted to hike. With her being a few months pregnant, we knew we didn't need anything too strenuous. We were looking forward to a little downtime in nature.

As we drove in, we stopped at a store to pick up some snacks, drinks, and some medicine. Both of us had itchy throats. It was nothing serious. But we wanted some Sudafed and cough drops just in case.

We arrived at the condo and immediately fell in love with the place. It was a one-bedroom, two story condo, with a loft. We had no internet, and no cell phone coverage. We didn't care. The view was stunning. Everything seemed perfect. Almost too perfect. It was too good to be true.

Kayci and I hadn't kept up with the weather, because that's not what we do on vacation. This was prior to social media, so there were no weather warnings coming across our news feeds on our devices. We were completely unaware that a snowstorm was about to blanket the top of our mountain. When I say blanket, I'm not talking inches. I'm talking feet. It dropped two feet of snow overnight. We woke up to over twenty-four inches of powdered snow. We were stuck. Snowed in. There would be no hiking. Our car was covered. The roads were closed.

And that wasn't even the worst part.

Kayci and I came down with the worst sinus infections either of us have ever had. Yet, we were snowed in. There was no way to get medicine, or get to a clinic. Not only that, there was no way to get more food. All we had were two big bags of Doritos, fish sticks, two boxes of mac and cheese, crackers, and squirt cheese. How we ended up with that selection, I'll never know. I'll take the blame. I was still in my mid-20s and thought it was a good idea. Please don't judge me.

We began rationing food and medicine. We had to figure out how we could make it last 3 days. On day 2 we ran out of Kleenexes and began going through rolls of toilet paper to blow our noses. At one point, I called my dad collect, hoping he would pick up the phone. Remember, we had no cell phone or internet connection. He picked up. I asked for him to put us on the prayer list at church. True story.

When we finally left the mountain, we stopped at the first corner store we passed. We were like Will Smith in the movie *Hitch* when he had an allergic reaction and began guzzling Benadryl, except we were downing Dayquil. Thankfully, we lived to tell the story.

Eating, drinking, and dining in the storm. It's not how we prefer to eat, live, fellowship, or celebrate. Yet, sometimes it's all we have.

***

Paul knew all about storms and navigating crises. He was a walking piece of conflict. Trouble seemed to follow him everywhere. Paul did not lack passion and motivation. When God caught a hold of his heart, Paul knew the only way to live—sold out for Jesus no matter what!

In 2 Corinthians 11, Paul shared about some of his trials, "Three times I was shipwrecked; for a night and a day I was adrift at sea."[23] That's nuts, right? And I'm not sure he's even referencing what may have been the worst story about him on a ship in a storm.

In Acts 27, Luke (the author), dedicates an entire chapter to Paul on a ship lost at sea. There were 276 people on the boat. That's a lot of people, which meant that must have been a big boat. They didn't have Dramamine. To continue, you may need to grab yours.

"Sailing was now dangerous." -Acts 27:9

"But soon a violent wind, called the northeaster, rushed down from Crete." -27:14

"We were scarcely able to get the ship's boat under control." -27:16

"We were being pounded by the storm so violently that on the next day they began to throw the cargo overboard." -27:19

---

[23] 2 Corinthians 11:25

"Neither sun nor stars appeared for many days." -27:20

"Since they had been without food for a long time..." -27:21

Basically, the people in charge wanted to get this boat to Rome, and they were determined to brave the elements to make it happen. Keep in mind, this wasn't a Royal Caribbean experience where people had their own rooms, beds to sleep in, and shelter from the storm. They were in it. It was wet, cold, and rainy. This is the *Deadliest Catch*, except they aren't catching crabs, but transporting prisoners.

On the boat and in the storm, Paul became a prophet, prayer leader, voice of reason, a calm presence, an encourager, and a leader. It didn't matter that Paul had prisoner status, God used him to help save the lives of 275 other people.

Paul became something else too. Paul became the host of a meal, and possibly, a priest or pastor presiding over The Lord's Table.

"Just before daybreak, Paul urged all of them to take some food, saying, "Today is the fourteenth day that you have been in suspense and remaining without food, having eaten nothing. Therefore I urge you to take some food, for it will help you survive; for none of you will lose a hair from your heads." ***After he had said this, he took bread; and giving thanks to God in the presence of all, he broke it and began to eat.*** Then all of them were encouraged and took food for themselves."[24]

---

[24] Acts 27:33-36.

They had been on a boat in the waves for days. They were hungry, fearful, and exhausted. Cargo had already been thrown over the sides of the boat.

And Paul took out bread and hosted a meal.

***

Having been a devout Jew, Paul grew up his entire life participating in the annual event called Passover. Participants in Passover retell the story of God delivering people from Egypt. It's not told like a story from the past. Language throughout the Passover is participatory, inclusive, and present-day language. It's not about "them" or "they," but "we" and "us." Throughout the Passover meal, there is also anticipation for God to bring ultimate deliverance and restoration through a Messiah.

I have taken part in a few Passover (also called *Seder*) meals over the past few years. It is one of the most meaningful events of the year for me. One of my favorite parts of the Passover meal is when the word *"Dayenu"* takes center stage. *Dayenu* means "it would have been enough," or "it is sufficient." It's a moment in the meal when we declare that even if God doesn't do anything else, what God has done for God's people is enough. I can't make it through this part of Passover without tearing up.

For Paul, there is a moment when he writes about God speaking this to him, "My grace is sufficient for you, for power is made perfect in weakness."[25] It sounds very much like *"dayenu."*

---

[25] 2 Corinthians 12:9.

Paul had been shaped by events like Passover. Then, beginning with his conversion in Acts 9, Paul had to have been introduced to the bread and the cup, or what some of us call The Lord's Table, Eucharist, communion, or The Lord's Supper.

In The Lord's Table, the church is reminded of the sacrifice of Jesus. The bread and the cup symbolize sacrifice, salvation, unity, and mission. For the early church, this wasn't a solemn event, but rather a highly participatory, communal event. It's a time the church remembers, celebrates, reenacts, and reminds itself of the story we have been invited into.

When Jesus broke bread, the Bible tells us that Jesus took it, blessed it, broke it, and gave it. Paul had been taught this. Paul would later go on to share the same message.

Maybe Acts 27 wasn't a communion service, but the language and meaning may have been fully present in Paul's intent. Paul wanted to do something for the people on the boat that day. He wanted to do something more than feed hungry bellies, but to nurture restless souls. He wanted people to connect with God.

***

For followers of Jesus, communion is an anchoring moment. At Sycamore View, we participate in this event every single week when we're together. Some think that taking communion weekly makes it lose its meaning. I'd argue that weekly communion reminds us every single week what the story is that we've been invited into. It reminds us that this story is greater than ourselves. It reminds us of the great sacrifice Jesus took upon Himself to connect us to God forever. It reminds us that Jesus' work through His death, burial, and resurrection means that God has accomplished something significant in and through Jesus. It is finished. Jesus has defeated sin and death forever. Yet, there is still work to be done.

The Lord's Table is about the past, present, and future. As we take the bread and the cup—this meal—we are reminded that God is asking God's people to live lives as people who are on mission. Because our hands and lips touch this bread and cup, we are commissioned by God to use our hands, lips, hearts, and lives to be a blessing to the world.

***

When our children were young, Kayci and I would often allow them to take the bread and the cup with us during church. Some parents choose not to let their children participate. For some, it's a rite of passage meant only for those who have declared their faith in Jesus through confession and baptism. I respect their decision. However, for Kayci and me, we used this time to have meaningful conversations with our children about Jesus' impact on the world. We used it as a teachable moment.

One Sunday, as we gave our kids the bread and the cup, one of our sons looked at me and asked, "Dad, can I have more?"

I knew in the moment he was asking for more of the bread. Yet, I couldn't help but pray, "God, he doesn't know what he is asking for right now. But I pray that this will be a request that will flow from his lips for the rest of his life."

"God, can I have more?"

Even through the storms that come at us in life, there needs to be a cry, "God, more of you. More of the bread. More of the cup. More of this reminder. More of this anchor."

For many years, the Jews celebrated Passover while the world around them was like a storm that raged. The night before Jesus was betrayed, Jesus celebrated Passover knowing He was within hours of dying a humiliating death. It was a storm that had been brewing since sin entered into the world. Many of us participate in The Lord's Table while storms are all around us, yet it is a meal meant to remind that there is a story that hovers over it all. Jesus invites us to eat even as we travel through the storms.

So, pull up a chair.

Take a seat.

Sit.

All are welcome.

Eat.

Enjoy.

OVERCOMING THE STORM OF DARKNESS

CHAPTER 8

I've cried in multiple messages I've delivered throughout my life. There are times I have told emotional stories or have spoken about the unfathomable love of God and tears have flowed. I don't hold in emotions very well.

Late 2018, Kayci and I traveled with a few dozen people to tour the Holy Lands. Our last day, we sat in a place of worship at The Garden Tomb. Some believe it is where the tomb of Jesus is located; therefore, it is where Jesus rose from the grave. Even if it isn't the exact location, we knew that we were within a mile of where the death, burial, and resurrection of Jesus took place.

We sang a few songs together, ending with *In Christ Alone*. Then, I stood up to speak about the significance of this location. I couldn't get words out. I was overcome by emotion. The words of *In Christ Alone* had wrecked me:

There in the ground His body lay, light of the world by darkness slain: Then bursting forth in glorious day, up from the grave He rose again.

Walking in and out of the tomb that would have been much like the one Jesus had been placed in, I was confronted with the truth that what God did for Jesus is what God will do for all of God's people. It's what God will do for all of creation. Kayci and I walked into the tomb together. We hugged and wept. As we walked out of the tomb, my mom was there to greet us. The three of us embraced as tears flowed. They weren't tears of sadness, but victory. The tears held pieces of grief, yet they were wrapped in great joy.

The death, burial, and resurrection of Jesus is the anchor of the Christian faith. This is what we said yes to in our baptisms. This was the event that changed history. The church wasn't founded on belief systems, worship styles, or doctrine, but on a person. A raised-from-death-to-life person.

This was the story my parents taught us to root ourselves in. It is the story that gave us courage to move forward after Jenny's death, because it reminded us that death will not win, and death will not get the last word. Our family anthem—*The Tomb is Empty*—is embedded in this reality. Jesus took on death head on, and He won.

There in The Garden Tomb, I stood and declared our faith in the God who raised Jesus from the dead. From the location where Jesus walked out of the grave, I talked about how we move forward in life refusing to be defined by anything that reflects death, but instead being defined by the adventurous life we're now invited into through an empty grave.

* * *

I wrote this book with hope in mind. As Hebrews says, "We have this hope as an anchor for the soul."[26] Jesus is our hope. Jesus isn't a heavenly life guard who hovers just close enough to catch us when we begin to go under. Jesus isn't a life insurance agent who is on call to help do damage control when we make a mess out of life. Jesus is an anchor. An anchor does nothing for us if we simply try to stay close by. You can see an anchor in the distance, yet it isn't useful or

---

[26] Hebrews 6:19.

helpful unless you are connected to it. The Bible talks about being rooted and grounded in Jesus, our anchor.[27]

Anchoring is about allegiance, properly directed adoration, and growing affections for Jesus. Throughout life, allegiance, adoration, and affections will constantly be challenged. There are multiple multi-billion-dollar industries that wage war against these things. Technology, entertainment, and cable news come for allegiance, adoration, and affections. When they replace Jesus as the anchor in our lives, we quickly become known by our fears, not our hopes. We also find ourselves susceptible to drifting, yet thinking we are fine in our faith because the anchor is in sight.

God never intended for us to be known more by what we fear in life than what we hope for. There is a better way God desires for us to live.

It all comes back to anchoring.

***

There's this moment during Jesus' crucifixion, in which we're given this interesting detail, "From noon until three in the afternoon darkness came over all the land."[28]

A storm was brewing. This storm had been raging since Genesis 3 and had now reached its climax. For three hours darkness came over the land during the time of day when light is often at its best. The human

---

[27] Ephesians 3:17.

[28] Matthew 27:45.

70

eyes of all the bystanders that day easily noticed what the gospel writers put into words; darkness hovered. However, the human eye was unable to see a storm raging in the unseen world.

The light of heaven and the darkness of evil had clashed. The sin of the world had been placed upon Jesus. This was a moment that Satan—the powers of darkness—felt that victory was within their reach. They had pinned down the Son of God. Darkness hovered, darkness penetrated, and darkness had wrapped itself around Jesus. The enemy thought darkness was leading to victory over the Messiah, yet God had other plans.

Most physical storms we experience in life have an element of darkness to them. Rain, hurricanes, thunderstorms, and tornadoes are often accompanied by darkness. Not only do storms create a darkness over the horizon as far as the human eye can see, but they carry the power to knock out electricity in the very places we attempt to take shelter from the storms. We keep candles and flashlights in specific locations in the house for this reason. Storms and darkness often go together.

Over 10% of Americans suffer from SADS—seasonal affective disorder syndrome. Darkness on the outside impacts how we feel on the outside. A few days of cloudy skies can lower morale, decrease energy, and negatively affect our psyche.

However, for God, darkness isn't a roadblock, but an opportunity for light to burst forth. Darkness can't hinder God's mission. Darkness can't outlast or outpower the light of God. Darkness wasn't able to permanently define Jesus, and darkness can't permanently define us either.

Darkness did have its way for a little while on that day. Darkness came over the land. Jesus suffered a horrible death on a Roman cross. God has directed wrath at sin. Sin had to be dealt with. To accomplish the mission, God trusted Jesus to complete it. God knew Jesus had the courage, heart, and passion to follow through with the mission of taking on the darkness of the world.

***

This wasn't the first time a storm of darkness preceded a mighty act of deliverance from God.

Many consider the narrative of deliverance found in the book of Exodus to be the greatest story of freedom in the Old Testament. God's people had been slaves for hundreds of years, and then God came and rescued the people from Egypt.

In the early chapters of Exodus, there are ten plagues. The tenth plague finally led to deliverance and freedom. It caused Pharaoh (the ruler of Egypt) to let the people go. However, the ninth plague was utter darkness. God brought darkness over the land. It wasn't just any darkness. Here's what we read, "Then the Lord said to Moses, 'Stretch out your hand over the sky so that darkness spreads over Egypt—*a darkness that can be felt.*' So Moses stretched out his hand toward the sky, and total *darkness covered all Egypt for three days.*"[29]

Deliverance from Egypt is arguably the greatest story of freedom in the Old Testament, but it's the death, burial, and resurrection of Jesus that is the greatest story of freedom in the Bible. Jesus brought

---

[29] Exodus 10:21-22.

an ultimate exodus that wasn't just good news for Egyptian slaves, but for all people.

In Egypt, a storm of darkness covered the land for three days. On a hill outside of Jerusalem, a storm of darkness covered the land for three hours. Neither storm of darkness set up permanent residence. The light of God always means freedom in God. Our God is not going to let darkness win.

You may feel like COVID-19 has created a storm of darkness that hovers over your life. You may feel as if darkness has set up residence in your life. It may feel like darkness is winning more battles in your life than it is losing.

Cling to your anchor. It tells you that there is a foundation that has been set, security that is in place, a war that has been won, and a light that will break through the dawn. Our anchor—Jesus—has weathered storms before, and He can do it again.

Jesus took the darkness of the entire world upon Himself. He carried it. He allowed it to overtake Him, because He knew that in the end, it would not have power over Him. Jesus trusted that in the dark, even in His death, that God would do everything God had promised to do. God wasn't going to leave him in the dark. God has no desire to leave us in the dark either.

Darkness may last for a season. But it's only a matter of time until the light of God breaks in.

Since Jesus took on death and darkness and won, what can't Jesus take on and win? If Jesus was able to defeat the storm of darkness and all its power, what storm can't Jesus defeat in your life?

***

73

This is the Easter story. God took on the storm of darkness and all the chaos darkness had unleashed upon the world, and through Jesus, dealt it a catastrophic blow.

The event of the death, burial, and resurrection of Jesus is more than a story that happened one day a couple thousand years ago. This is where we sometimes miss the impact of the Easter story. It's not a moment in history. It's an event that is still performing. It's not a story to be applauded as much as it's a story to step into to claim as our own.

Nothing anchors our faith more than the story of Jesus defeating death and walking out of a grave. Paul said it like this, "And if Christ has not been raised, our preaching is useless and so is your faith."[30] For Paul, and every New Testament writer, the story of Jesus rising from the dead is more than a part of our faith, it is the foundation for it.

The death, burial, and resurrection of Jesus calls for a response. I'd even go as far to say that it demands a response. When we surrender our lives to Jesus and place our faith in Him, we are converted into a movement. Our baptisms are more than a moment in time; they are an initiation into a new, adventurous life.

Every single year, Easter should be a season that anchors us again. It should center us. It should cause us to deeply reflect upon our lives, and to make changes—sometimes radical changes—to how we are living our lives for the glory of God.

---

[30] 1 Corinthians 15:14.

This life we are invited into is more than an obligation, it is a privilege. It is more than an invitation to be a fan of Jesus, but a devout, courageous follower.

Much of my work is to help people anchor properly, and sometimes that includes convincing people that they're anchoring to the wrong things.

You can't anchor in fear and hope at the same time.

You can't anchor in a political party and to the Kingdom of God at the same time.

You can't anchor in a family a member, a spouse, a friend, or a mentor as your source of fulfillment, security, and dependence.

You can't anchor in the promise of next year, next job, or next house.

You can't anchor in money, pensions, or retirement plans.

False and temporary anchors are all around us. Resist them. Know that they will never permanently satisfy. Don't bank on them. Don't trust in them. Know that they will let you down.

Anchor in Jesus.

He's the anchor we can trust.

He's the anchor that gives victory over every storm.

He's the anchor that ignites courage.

He's the anchor that cultivates a deep, abiding life in God.

The storms of life can have their way with us, but we don't have to be defined by them. Not when we're anchored.

***

In his masterful book, *What's So Amazing About Grace?*, Philip Yancey tells the story about the volcanic eruption of Mt. St. Helens. After the eruption, it left behind a thick mantle of ash. As with every volcano, the naturalists of the Forest Service began to wonder how long it would take before any living thing would grow there again. Then it happened. A park employee came across a patch of wildflowers, ferns, and grasses rooted to a strip of desolation.

Yancey tells the story like this, "It took a few seconds for him to notice an eerie fact: this patch of vegetation formed the shape of an elk. Plants had sprouted from the organic material that lay where an elk had been buried by ash. From then on, the naturalist looked for such patches of luxuriance as an aid in calculating the loss of wildlife."[31]

From death, life sprung forth.

Easter gives life to you. It gives life to the church. It gives life to the world.

Anchoring in Jesus doesn't lead to complacency or apathy.

Anchoring in Jesus isn't boring or stale.

Anchoring in Jesus gives birth to truth, courage, hope, and joy.

---

[31] Philip Yancey, *What's So Amazing about Grace?* (Grand Rapids, MI: Zondervan, 1997), 253.

Anchoring in Jesus doesn't prevent the storms in life from raging, but it promises security as we walk through them.

Anchoring in Jesus isn't just about you holding on to Him, but it's knowing that He is hanging on to you.

Made in the USA
Monee, IL
29 January 2021